VICTORIA AND ALBERT MUSEUM

Musical Instruments
as works of art

Peter Thornton

HER MAJESTY'S STATIONERY OFFICE

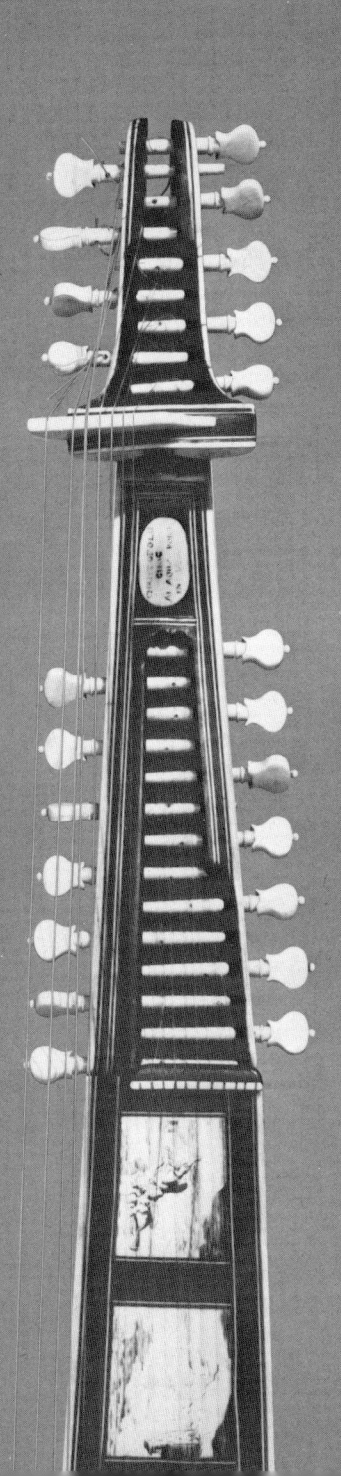

Preface

Our world today is filled with music which can be obtained at the flick of a switch. We may be delighted by it but, by and large, we take it for granted. Until about 1600, however, an instrument that could produce musical sounds was regarded as almost magical, an object to treasure and treat with enormous respect. At the same time the ability to read musical notation was reserved for an élite, and the study of the properties of strings under tension, and the sounds they could produce in varying circumstances, was considered a proper activity for the members of academies of science. While peasant bands might make music for the rural population, and jugglers or mummers might entertain the city-dweller with accompaniment on musical instruments of the cruder sort, the owning and playing of instruments that produced sweet sounds was largely confined to people of learning and discrimination. The instruments they owned were kept and displayed with pride, usually in one of the innermost rooms of a house alongside other treasured possessions. Because musical instruments were frequently to be seen among other highly ornamental objects, they were often elaborately decorated. Indeed, the larger pieces, notably harpsichords and spinets, were often embellished so as to fit in with the general *décor* of the rooms in which they were to stand.

Musical instruments continued to be regarded with considerable veneration until well into the eighteenth century, and it was only towards 1800 that most of the forms became stereotyped, very much as we know them today. Thenceforward, while shapes might still be attractive, decoration was kept to a minimum. It is really only the piano that has continued to be decorated to conform with current tastes right through to the present day, since it is so large a piece of furniture that it is required to blend with its surroundings.

The illustrations in this picture book are all of instruments in the Victoria and Albert Museum. As this is principally a museum of decorative arts, many of the instruments in its extremely important collection have been acquired especially on account of their decorative qualities. It is therefore appropriate that the Museum should draw special attention to this aspect of its collection. When I compiled the first edition of this picture book in 1967, I hoped to stimulate interest in this subject, but I had not anticipated the enormous explosion of interest that has since taken place in musicology and the study of ancient musical instruments. With it there has arisen a demand for information about the decoration of instruments, mainly from those people, mostly quite young, who are today making reproductions of old instruments. This will surely provide an incentive for scholars to take up the study more seriously. As yet the field has hardly been explored, and it is hoped that the present entirely revised edition of this largely pictorial offering will help to stimulate such exploration.

It would also be rewarding if students of antique furniture and woodwork were to pay greater attention to decorated musical instruments, for the simple reason that most instruments are inscribed with both date and provenance. Such firmly documented specimens are hard to come by in related fields. Musical instruments can, for instance, throw light on the provenance of jewel caskets and small boxes decorated in a manner similar to that of various sixteenth-century spinets and harpsichords. Anyone interested in the early history of marquetry ought at least to look at the decorated fingerboards of seventeenth-century Paduan and Venetian lutes. And no student of decorative painting can afford to ignore keyboard instruments which have throughout the centuries provided a vehicle for the display of the painter's talents. In the same way, musical instruments can provide important points of reference for the historical study of the adoption of moresque ornament in sixteenth-century Italy, or the use of grotesque patterns in eighteenth-century Germany, or the early use of ornamental paper embellishment.

It may be necessary for reasons of conservation to segregate ancient musical instruments in special rooms on their own, but they ought ideally to be seen amid other works of decorative art from their periods. Since they are themselves objects of great beauty and delicacy, they add to the glamour of the objects among which they are placed, and our understanding of them is in turn enhanced by their being seen in a wider context.

P K Thornton
Keeper
Department of Furniture and Woodwork

Printed in England for Her Majesty's Stationery Office
by Staples Printers St Albans Limited at The Priory Press
Dd 696331 C85

Figure 1
By the middle of the sixteenth century Italian keyboard instruments were being decorated in a comparatively ambitious manner, as this spinet made in Milan in 1555 shows. The keyboard is surrounded by delicate carving in the characteristic Renaissance idiom. The front of the case is inlaid with stringing and lozenges in a style often found on Italian boxes and carcase-furniture of the period. Note the small ivory studs set in the top edge of the casing, a common feature of Italian keyboard instruments at this time.
Spinet by Annibale dei Rossi, Milan, 1555; Museum No.156-1869.

Figure 2
An Italian spinet of the same period (dated 1568) but decorated with elaborate painted and gilded scrollwork. The recessed arcading on the fronts of the keys was a common feature on sixteenth-century Italian keyboards.
Spinet made by a certain Francesco of Brescia but inscribed with the name of Marco Iadra who was perhaps a dealer in musical instruments; Museum No.155-1869.

3

3a

4

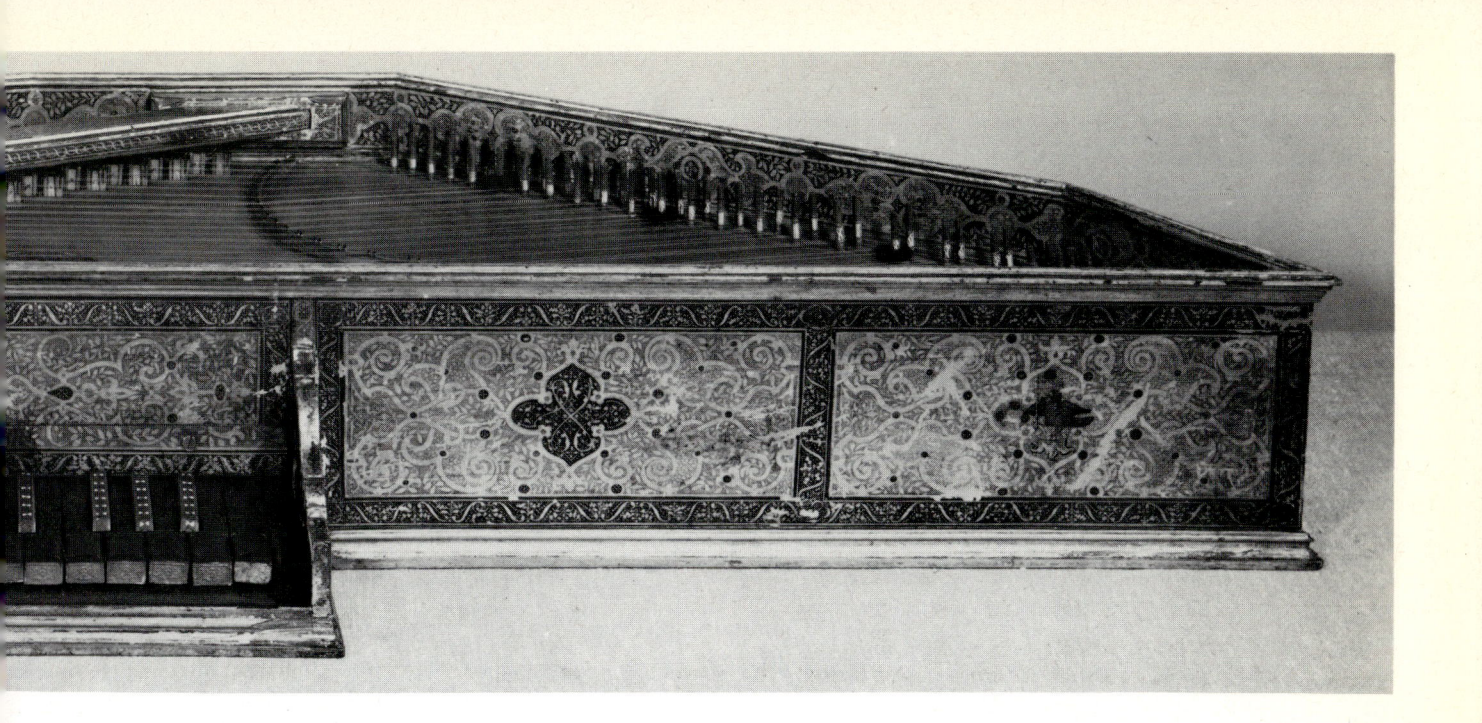

Figures 3 and 3a
An Italian instrument with particularly magnificent decoration; a spinet made about 1570, probably in Venice. It carries the English royal arms as borne by the Tudor monarchs (Fig.3) and the badge sported by Queen Anne Boleyn and her daughter Queen Elizabeth (Fig.3a). It must have belonged to the latter and has indeed been known as 'Queen Elizabeth's Virginals', at least since the eighteenth century. The arabesque decoration is executed in transparent tinted varnish over a gold ground, the pattern being reserved in gold (i.e. the ground is coloured, the pattern being left in unobscured gold). This seems to have been a favourite method of decorating expensive articles (boxes, furniture, etc.) in the late sixteenth and early seventeenth centuries.
'*Queen Elizabeth's Virginals*', *Venice about 1570; Museum No.19-1887.*

Figures 4, 4a and 4b
Details of the decoration of another very elaborate Italian spinet. Made by Annibale dei Rossi in Milan in 1577, it is ornamented with strapwork cartouches of ivory on panels of ebony, set with some 1,900 semi-precious stones – garnets, turquoises, lapis-lazuli, etc. In spite of all this sumptuous embellishment, the instrument has a most pleasing tone. It may well be with reference to this very instrument that an Italian writer in 1595 stated that 'Annibale Rosso was worthy of praise ... This skilful maker constructed among other works a clavichord of uncommon beauty and excellence, with keys all of precious stones, and with the most elegant ornaments. This instrument was sold for 500 crowns, and is now in the possession of the learned and refined gentleman, Signor Carlo Trivulzio'. Certainly an instrument like this would have been highly prized both as an instrument and for its ornament; it was very probably kept among other treasures in a closet, a Cabinet of Curiosities.
Spinet by A. dei Rossi, Milan, 1577; Museum No.809-1869.

Figure 5
The keyboard area of a Venetian harpsichord of 1574 decorated with a gilt moresque pattern on black. The section of lid above is seen again in Figure 5a.

Figure 5b
The roses of many Italian instruments (both keyboard and stringed) continued to be decorated with Gothic tracery long after this style had been abandoned for ornamenting other parts of the instruments. Figure 5b shows the rose of a Venetian harpsichord of 1574 which is decorated in all other respects in an entirely fashionable style (see Fig.5 and 5a). The Rossi spinet of 1577 (see Fig.4) is remarkable because its rose (Fig.4a) is ornamented in the contemporary taste.

Figure 5a
The painted decoration inside the lid of the protective case provided for the Venetian harpsichord of 1574. The tail end of the instrument has been truncated so the decoration there is cut away. Very few such outer cases of the period have survived.

6

6a

Figures 6 and 6a
The painted decoration on a charming miniature Italian spinet of about 1600. The board above the keys is delicately decorated with figures in arcading, executed in gold on a black ground (Fig.6a). Some painted draperies, added (probably during the last century) to hide the nakedness of the mermaids, were removed when the instrument was restored in 1964.
Spinetino, about 1600; Museum No.218-1870.

Figures 7 and 7a
The carved exterior of a Flemish virginal of 1568 made for the Duke of Cleves. The outside of this instrument, rectangular in plan, is treated like a piece of carcase furniture, such as a chest, and is embellished with Italianate Mannerist decoration like that often seen on the fronts of buffets and ornamental cupboards. It was probably made at Antwerp, which was to become the most important centre for the making of keyboard instruments in the first half of the seventeenth century.
Virginal, Antwerp (?), 1568; Museum No.447-1896.

Figures 8 and 8a
The painted case of a claviorganum made in 1579 by an important Flemish instrument maker working in London. The decoration, which is very competent, is a reminder that much sixteenth-century furniture was painted, and that work of this class would have constituted a striking feature of any fashionable Tudor interior.
Combined organ and harpsichord by Lodewijk Theewes, London, 1579; Museum No.125-1890.

Figures 9 and 9a
The elegant body of a lute made at Padua in 1592 by one of the most famous lutemakers of his day, Wendelin Tieffenbrucker. Among the leading lutemakers working in Italy at this period were a number of Germans. German craftsmanship in wood reached a high degree of excellence at this time. Note the subtle use of naturally shaded wood to stress the ribbed construction of the body, and the panels of marquetry on the neck, here executed with veneers of ebony and ivory. This latter was an advanced technique at this date. The rose (Fig.9a), on the other hand, with its elaborate interlacing, is a reminder of the lute's Near Eastern origins.
Lute by Wendelin Tieffenbrucker, Padua, 1592; converted into a chittarone in the eighteenth century; Museum No.W.6-1940.

Figure 10
The triple rose of a chittarone made in 1614 by another German, Matteo Buechenberg, who worked in Rome. Note the Arabic character of the interlaced pattern. This instrument bears the Medici arms surmounted by a grand-ducal crown, which suggests that it was originally used by a musician attached to the court of Cosimo II, Grand Duke of Tuscany. As Buechenberg was the most famous of the early makers of the chittarone, this seems entirely plausible.
Chittarone by Matteo Buechenberg, Rome, 1614; Museum No.190-1882.

Figure 11
The triple rose of another Buechenberg instrument, the patterns here deriving from the Gothic tradition.
Theorbo by Matteo Buechenberg, Rome, 1619; Museum No.218-1882.

Figure 12
The rose of a lute made in Siena in 1621 with an interlace of Islamic inspiration.
Lute by Andrea Taus, Siena, 1621; subsequently converted into a chittarone; Museum No.5989-1859.

Figure 13
The rose of a theorbo made in Venice in 1637. The tracery is once again Gothic.
Theorbo by Matteo Sellas, Venice, 1637; Museum No.1126-1869.

Figure 14
The back of a Venetian guitar, made in 1623 for the Grand Duke Ferdinand of Tuscany. The unusual overall zig-zag pattern is skilfully worked in ivory and ebony. Note the scrollwork marquetry on the neck.
Guitar by Matteo Sellas, Venice, 1623; Museum No.7356-1861.

Figure 15
A more common form of decoration for the body of a guitar is shown here. It consists of fluted ribs with ivory stringing. The marquetry on the neck is of an identical pattern to that of the previous example and they were probably both made in the same workshop.
Guitar, probably by Matteo Sellas, Venice, about 1625; Museum No.390-1871.

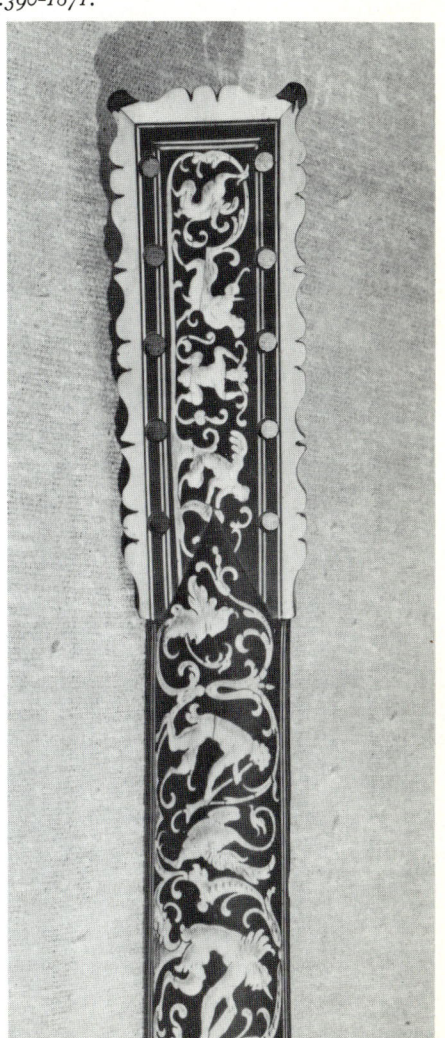

Figure 16
The neck of a fine Venetian guitar dated 1627. The marquetry of ivory and ebony is delicately engraved.
Guitar-neck by Giogio Sellas, Venice, 1627; Museum No.358-1896.

Figure 17
The carved body of a Parisian instrument apparently dated 1610. It is here shown approximately full size. The representation of the Three Graces is in the style of the Fontainebleau School and one might have guessed that the carving was executed in the mid 1500s, but the date minutely inscribed on the instrument belies this. In fact the style remained in favour well into the next century. *Mandore by Boissart, Paris, 1610, or just possibly 1640, the third figure being unclear; Museum No.219-1866.*

Figure 18
An example of decoration taking over an instrument entirely. The whole of the inside of this virginal is faced with glass ornaments. Shown here are some of the scenes executed in coloured glass set inside the lid. It can never have been a practicable musical instrument but no doubt was a greatly prized treasure in some *Wunderkammer*. It is said to have belonged to Elizabeth, Queen of Bohemia, the daughter of James I. However, an instrument 'made all of glass, except for the strings' was seen at Hampton Court by a German visitor in 1598, so it is possible that the instrument shown here first belonged to Queen Elizabeth of England before becoming the property of the other Elizabeth, 'The Winter Queen'. The origin of the coloured glass elements is much disputed by experts on ancient glass. While such glass originally came from Murano, near Venice, it was later produced in France, Flanders and Germany. The shape of the virginal is, however, Italian. *Virginal, late sixteenth or early seventeenth century; Museum No.402-1872.*

18

Figures 19 and 19a
A small spinet fitted into an elaborate case of ebony decorated with silver strapwork ornament and engraved and enamelled plaques. The box can also serve as a writing-desk; it has a compartment with a sliding top in the lid and a secret drawer in the base. This is characteristic of the expensive confections of ebony and silver created by Augsburg silversmiths during the late sixteenth century and the first half of the seventeenth. Such *cabinets d'Allemagne* were greatly prized all over Europe and were favoured as princely gifts. Many could serve more than one purpose, as in this instance. Although it must be regarded largely as a toy, the instrument works remarkably well.
Octave-spinet, Augsburg, about 1600;
Museum No.4265-1857.

Figures 20 and 20a
A positive organ made in Saxony about 1625. Included in the *decoupé* card decoration masking the ends of the pipes is a portrait of Johan Georg I, Duke of Saxony. This small instrument is treated like a cabinet, the inside of the doors being painted with Biblical scenes. Note the strapwork cresting so characteristic of the Northern Renaissance style favoured all over Germany at this period.
Positive organ probably made in Dresden by Gottfried Fritzsche, organ-maker to the Electoral Court of Saxony, about 1625 (possibly in 1627);
Museum No.2-1867.

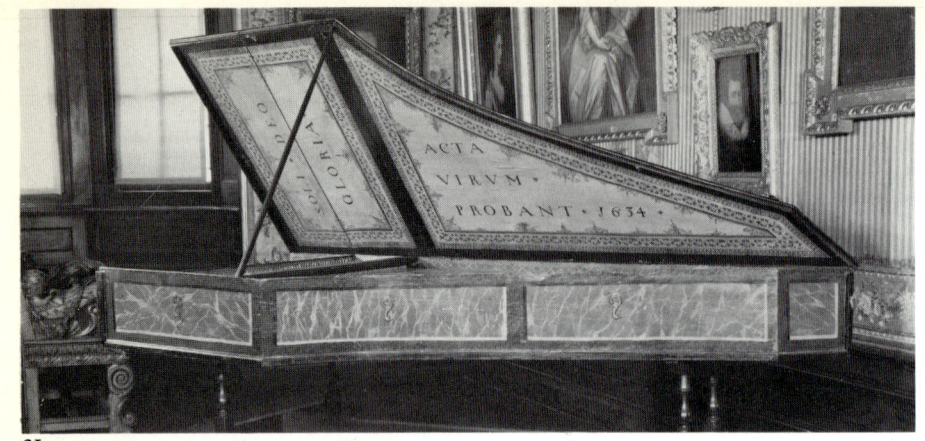

Figures 21 and 21a
The important harpsichord at Ham House (a property which is administered by the Victoria and Albert Museum) is inscribed *Joannes Ruckers me fecit Antwerpiae* and is dated 1634. Notwithstanding the inscription, it may well be an English instrument of the eighteenth century, but it is decorated in the typical Flemish seventeenth-century manner – marbled on the outside and with the interior ornament executed entirely with printed papers (even the graining is printed, as are the border-strips, etc.). Figure 21a shows the 'dolphin paper' round the keyboard, which was so characteristic a feature of instruments made by the famous Ruckers workshops at Antwerp. The firm's output was enormous and the Flemish makers adopted this form of embellishment (Ruckers used several variants of the 'dolphin-paper', for instance, and other firms had their own house patterns) as part of a programme of rationalisation. So excellent were Flemish instruments of this period that they continued in favour until the second half of the eighteenth century, and many eighteenth-century harpsichord-makers obtained substantial business in extending and modernising ancient Flemish instruments. The present example appears, however, to be a completely new instrument, created around 1730 in England to meet the demand for reconditioned Flemish harpsichords. Although details of the decoration are not completely accurate, the result has been sufficiently plausible to remain unsuspected until quite recently.
Harpsichord probably made in London about 1730; Museum No.H.H.109.

Figure 21b
The gilt rose of the Ham House instrument is of cast metal with the initials of Jan Ruckers. The soundboard is painted with naturalistic flowers in the characteristic Flemish manner. Whoever made this pastiche (which is an excellent instrument in its own right) was clearly entirely familiar with genuine Ruckers decoration.

Figure 22
The making of keyboard instruments had not been long established in this country when this virginal was constructed (1642). Although it has a remarkably good tone, the robust case-work is of no great distinction and its embellishment is simple. Strips of embossed gilt paper are used to trim the keyboard surround. This was a device much used by Flemish instrument-makers (traces are to be found on the Theewes harpsichord and the Duke of Cleves' virginals, Figures 7 and 8), it was also adopted for the frames of the small alabaster reliefs which were produced in large quantities in Malines at this period.
Virginal by Thomas White, London, 1642; Museum No.W.1-1933.

Figure 23
The outer case provided in the seventeenth century for an Italian harpsichord of 1521, its original case having presumably become unserviceable by this time. It is covered with leather, exquisitely tooled and gilded in a manner that is more usually to be seen on book-bindings. It is uncommon to find articles of tooled leather of such a large size.
Harpsichord case, probably Roman, seventeenth century; Museum No.226-1879.

Figure 24
The inside of the outer case provided during the second half of the seventeenth century for 'Queen Elizabeth's Virginals' (Fig.3). The outside is faced with red velvet, while the inside is decorated with a fairly close imitation in black and gold of Japanese lacquer work. Even the ground is powdered with gold dust in imitation of a favourite Japanese technique of the period. It is curious that such an exotic form of decoration should have been considered suitable for an instrument case, but perhaps Queen Elizabeth's Virginals were regarded, already in the late seventeenth century, as a rarity fit to be displayed, like Japanese lacquer and its imitations, in a *Wunderkammer*.
Case for a virginal, English, second half of the seventeenth century; Museum No.12a-1887.

24

Figures 25 and 25a
A dancing-master's fiddle (also known as a *pochette*, because such small instruments could fit into a pocket in the large-skirted suits of the time) made in Paris during the third quarter of the seventeenth century. The *coiffure* of the woman's head forming the finial indicates the date; the gilt tooling of the red leather case is also consonant with such a date. The tooled motifs include crowned Ls and a crowned dolphin, which presumably allude to Louis, the Grand Dauphin (1661-1711), the eldest son of Louis XIV. The dancing-master who used this small fiddle must therefore have been in the Dauphin's service and the young prince was probably given his early lessons in manners, deportment and the principal dance-steps to tunes played on this charming little instrument which itself exhibits craftsmanship of the highest quality.
Pochette by Dimanche Drouyn, Paris, 1660s; Museum No. 51-1872.

25

25a

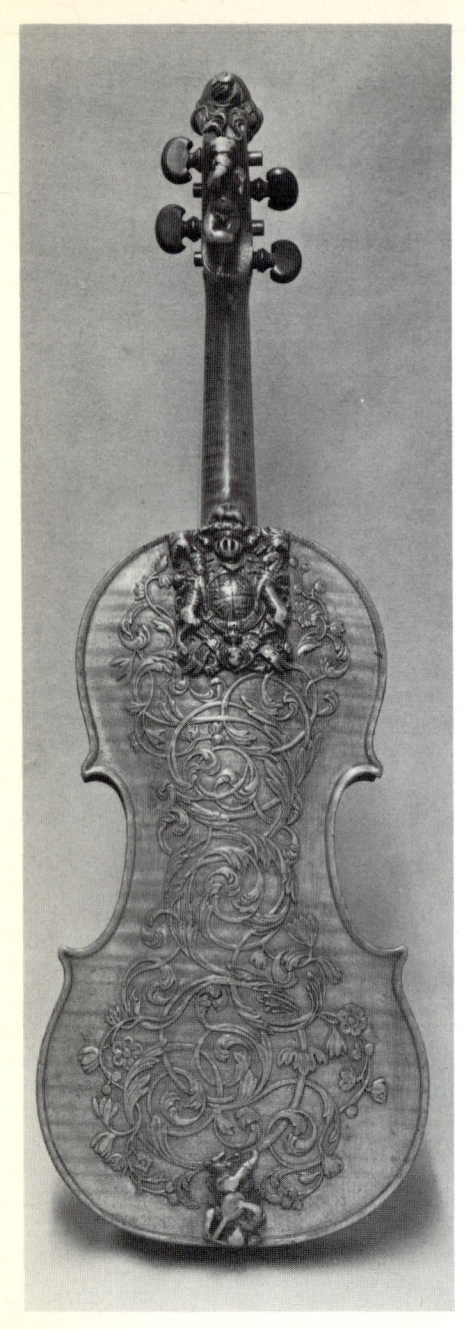

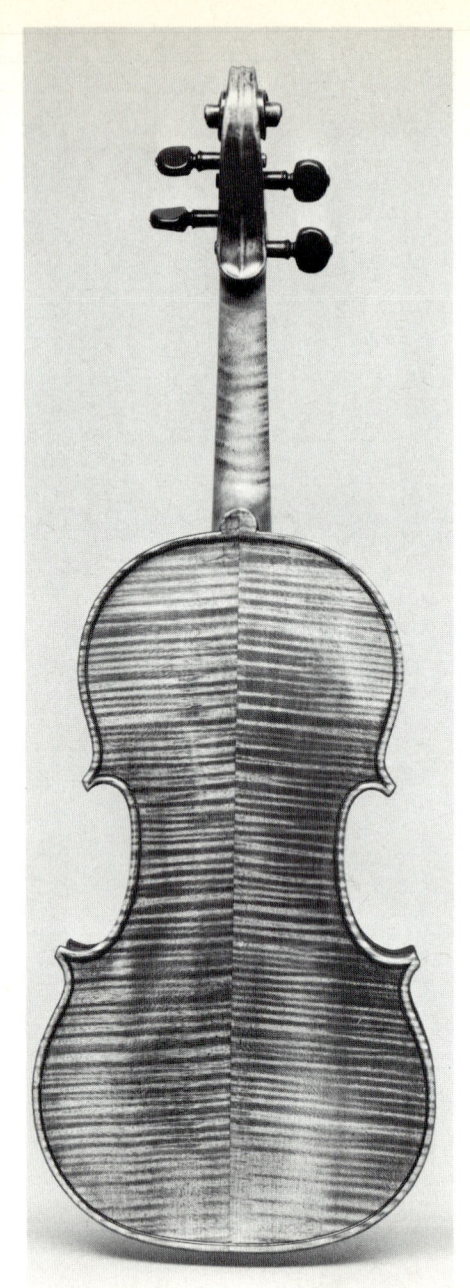

Figure 26
A violin skilfully carved with scrollwork of a most lively conception, and with the English royal arms as borne by Charles II and James II: it must therefore date from between 1660 and 1688. Unfortunately the identity of the maker of this outstanding instrument is not at present known.
Violin, English, about 1670?; Museum No.34-1869.

Figure 27
A violin by the famous maker Antonio Stradivari of Cremona, dated 1699. The craft of violin-making is generally held to have reached its summit at this small North Italian town towards the end of the seventeenth century, and especially in the hands of Stradivari, but it is not easy to explain why this should have been the case. The special virtues of the best Cremonese work lie in the choice of wood, the subtle detailing, the excellent finish, and the elegance of the forms. The shape which had been evolved for the purpose was deemed sufficiently beautiful in itself not to require additional ornament in the form of applied carving or marquetry, and it is a reflection of the self-assurance of the Cremonese craftsmen that, in the Baroque period when it was normal for works of art (including musical instruments) to be richly decorated, they left their instruments unembellished with additional ornament. Having perfected an instrument that performed its task most admirably, the Cremonese masters were content to allow the form thus evolved to speak for itself.
Violin by Antonio Stradivari, Cremona, 1699; Museum No.W.104-1937. The instrument has been re-necked.

Figures 28 and 28a
In contrast to the Cremonese violin mentioned above, this sumptuously decorated instrument displays the Baroque love of full-blooded ornament, which instrument-makers at the time were accustomed to apply. This baryton, an instrument rather larger than a cello, lent itself particularly well to such treatment.
Baryton by Joachim Tielke, Hamburg, 1686; Museum No.115-1865.

Figure 29
The rose of a German cittern, which dates from the late seventeenth or early eighteenth century but still embodies forms of Gothic origin. The conservatism evinced in the design of roses for musical instruments is extraordinary.
Cittern, German, about 1700; Museum No.35-1867.

Figure 30
The bell of a Dutch oboe carved with figures of musicians dressed in the late seventeenth-century fashion. The legs of the table also indicate a Dutch provenance and a seventeenth-century date.
Oboe stamped 'Beukers', Dutch, late seventeenth century; Museum No.808-1869.

'Queen Elizabeth's Virginals', Venice, about 1570; Museum No.19-1887.
See figure 3.

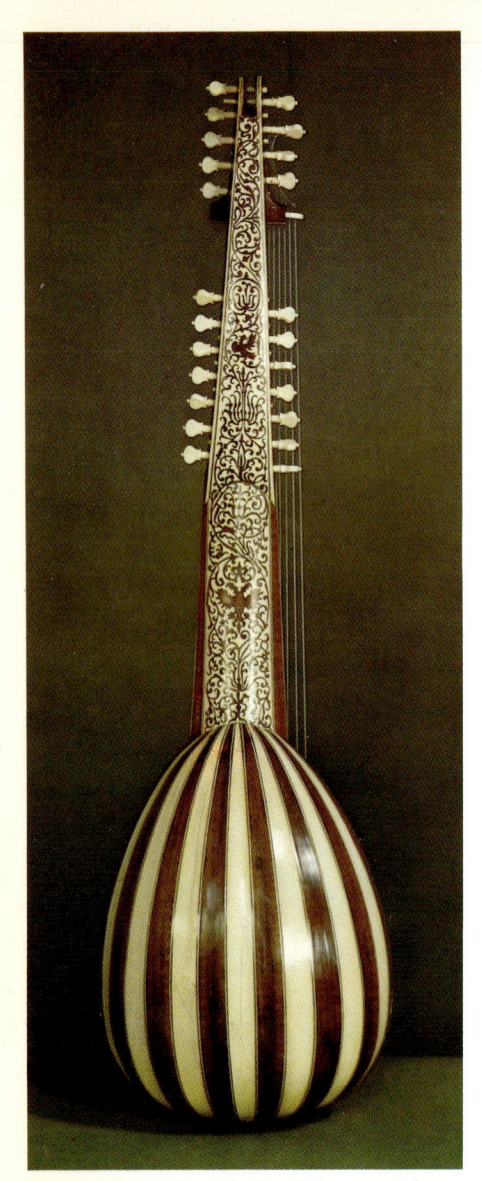

Theorbo by 'Cristofolo Choc' (presumably
Christofer Koch), Venice, mid-seventeenth
century; Museum No.7756-1862.

Pochette by Dimanche Drouyn, Paris, 1660's;
Museum No.519-1872.
See figure 25.

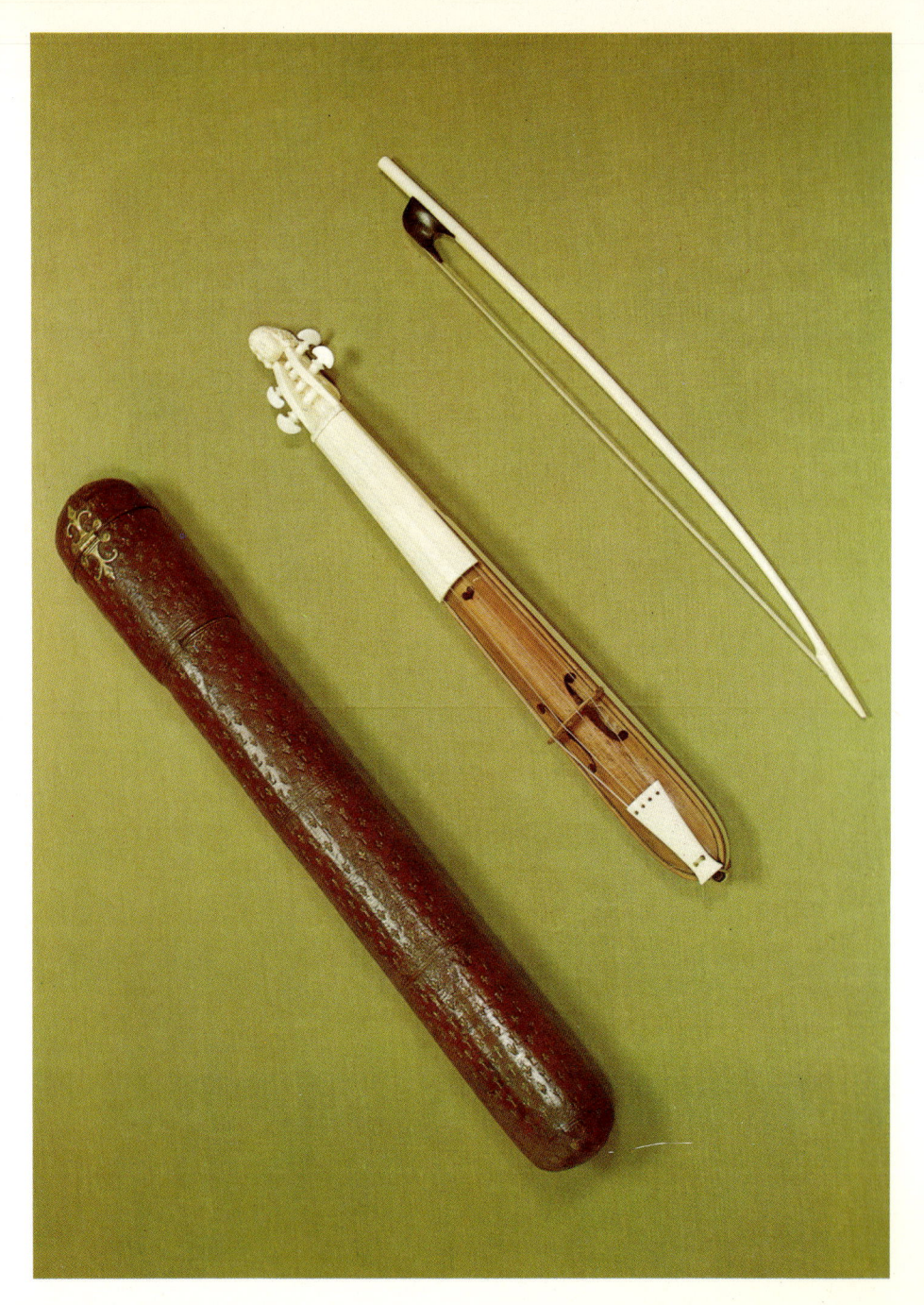

This instrument was made by an instrument-maker who served the French Court, and its fine exterior decoration can be taken to reflect the best that was available in Paris at the time. What is intended as chinoiserie decoration (executed in gold and silver on a black ground) in imitation of Oriental lacquer is in fact based on engravings of European subjects (eg peasants returning from work by Jacques Stella). Dated Japanned decoration is of course very rare. The red and gold chinoiseries inside the lid date from the early 18th century.
Harpsichord by Antoine Vaudry, Paris, 1681; Museum No.W.12-1974.

Bass viol by Martin Voigt, Hamburg, 1726; Museum No.1298-1871.
See figure 39.

The inside of the bell of this elegant instrument is decorated with a garland of oak-leaves reversed on a green lacquer ground. The brass surface thus provides the gold for the garland and can be seen through the green lacquer.
French horn by Marcel-Auguste Raoux, Paris, about 1826; Museum No.W.83-1926.

31

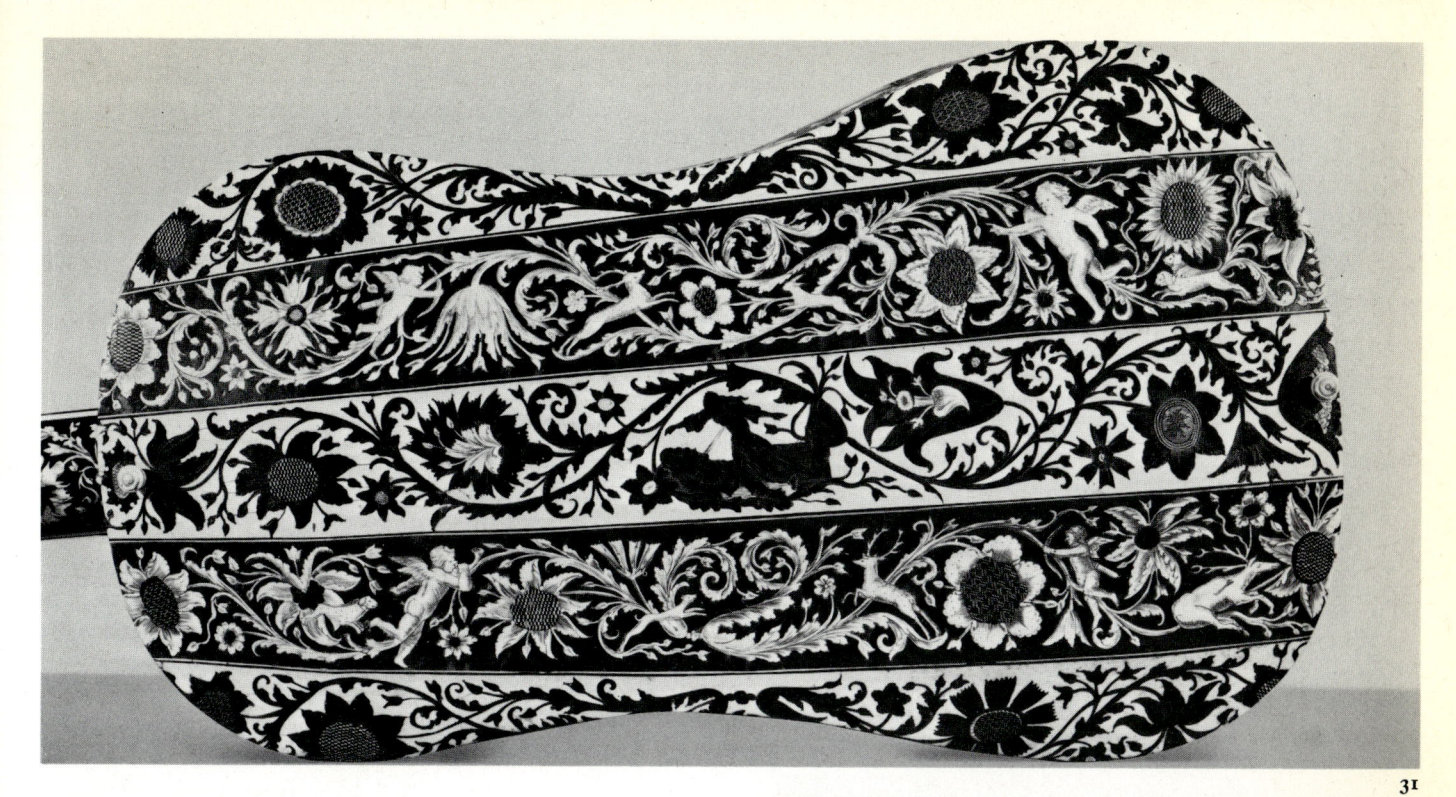

Figures 31, 31a and 31b, 31c over page
One of the most ambitious – and successful – essays in decorating a musical instrument with marquetry ornament. It is executed in ivory and tortoiseshell with engraved detailing, enhanced with passages rendered in pewter.
The peg-box (Fig.31c) showing the laminated edges, the chequered scrollwork through which the decorative pegs are set, and the charming open-work filling is especially remarkable. The astonishingly intricate rose of the guitar (Fig.31a), is made of cut card, partly gilded, and

31a

31c

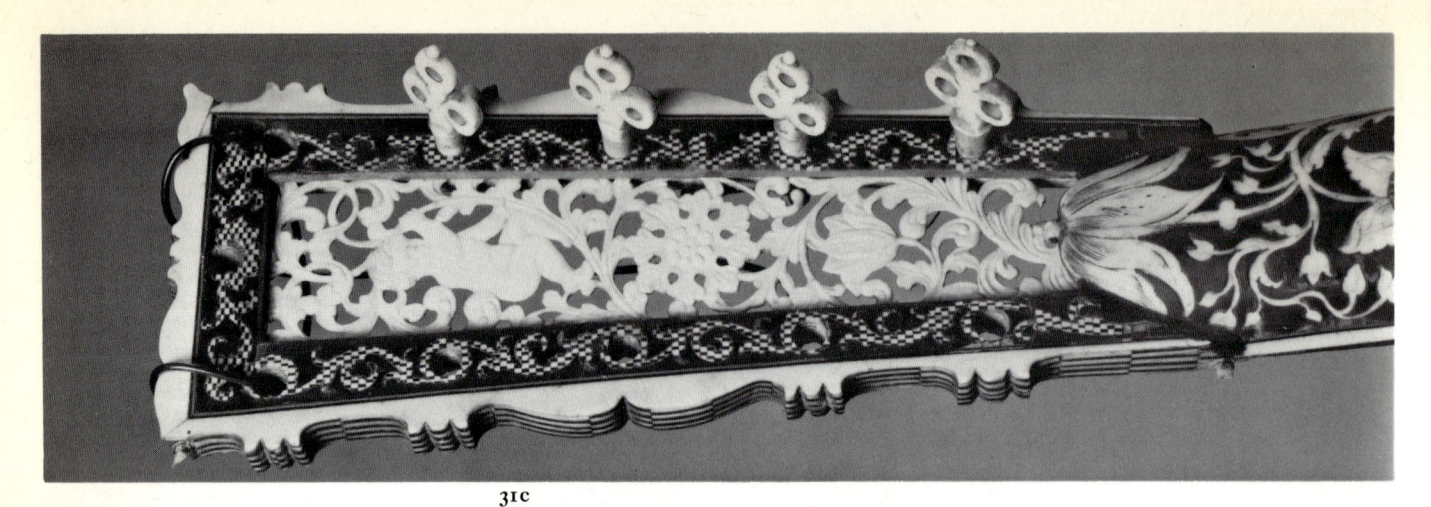

descends in several tiers into the body. It is noteworthy once again that the cut-out patterns of the rose still retain their traditional Gothic form, even at this late date and on an instrument otherwise decorated in the most up-to-date manner. *Guitar by Joachim Tielke, Hamburg, 1693; Museum No.676-1872.*

31b

Figure 32
Another elegant instrument from the Tielke workshops at Hamburg. Here the shape of the body is merely accented by ivory edging, and the ornament is confined to the fingerboard and neck.
Bass viol by Joachim Tielke, Hamburg, early eighteenth century; Museum No.7360-1861.

Figure 33
Italian makers of keyboard instruments habitually provided them with painted cases, and special attention was usually paid to the decoration inside the lid. The painting was sometimes of excellent quality, as in the present example, a lid apparently painted in Venice about 1720. The scene is the *Judgment of Midas*. It is distressing that only the lid has survived of what must have been an important and beautiful instrument.
(Museum No.444-1887).

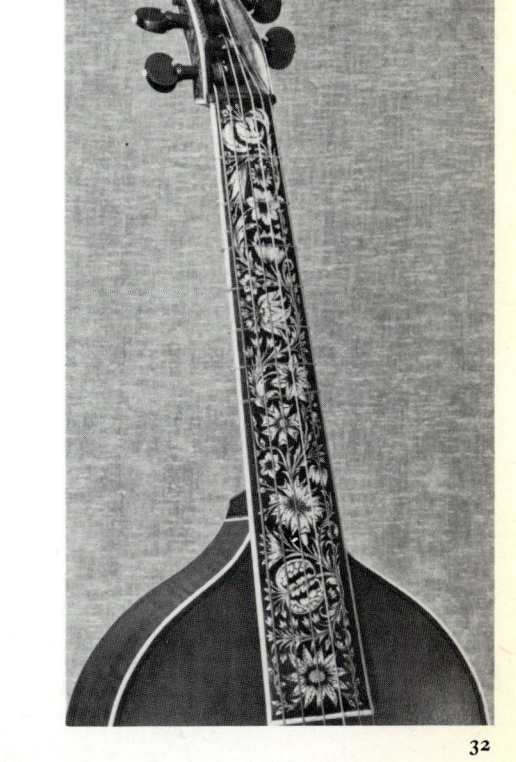

31

Figure 34
An Italian dulcimer, the protective case of which is painted in much the same manner as Italian keyboard-instruments of the period – about 1700.
Dulcimer, Italian, about 1700;
Museum No.4-1869.

35 35a

Figures 35 and 35a
The bell of a carved ivory oboe made in Milan early in the eighteenth century. The instrument later belonged to Rossini.
Oboe by J. M. Anciuti of Milan, early eighteenth century; Museum No.1127-1869.

Figure 36
A Baroque flute of ebony inlaid with silver in the French style. The maker, P. J. Bressan, was working in London, but was presumably of French extraction.
Flute by P. J. Bressan, London, about 1710; Museum No.542-1898.

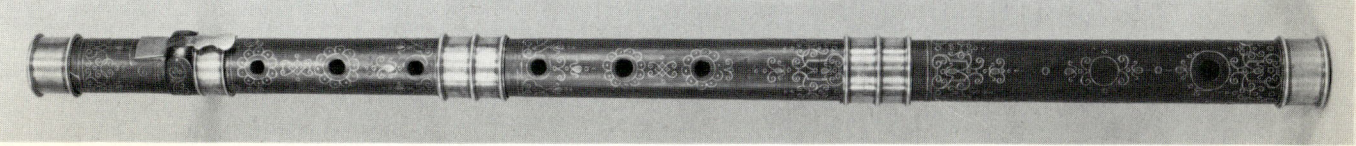

36

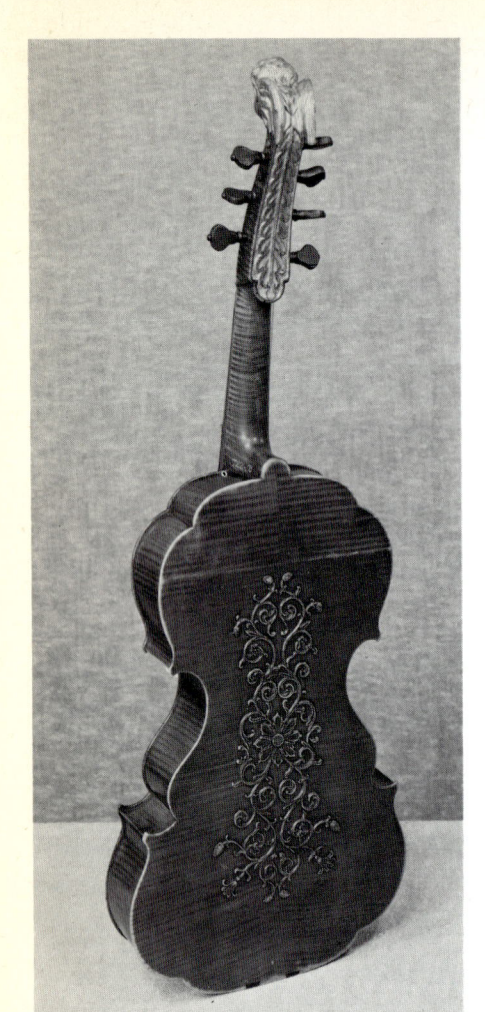

Figure 37
The decorated back of a South German viola d'amore which is said to be dated 1719. It bears the arms of Franz Anton, Graf von Harrach, Prince-Bishop of Salzburg (1708-27). The finial is in the form of a gilded angel's head. The 'festooned' shape of the body was much favoured for viols in Germany during the Baroque period.
Viola d'amore, South German, 1719; Museum No.732-1878.

Figure 38
The rich ornament of a German baryton of about 1720. It bears the name of Jacques Sainprae of Berlin who may have been its owner rather than the maker. The instrument must have been made by a follower of Joachim Tielke of Hamburg (see Fig.31). The carving is of outstanding quality. Note the small mask on the side of the neck.
Baryton, North German, about 1720; Museum No.1444-1870.

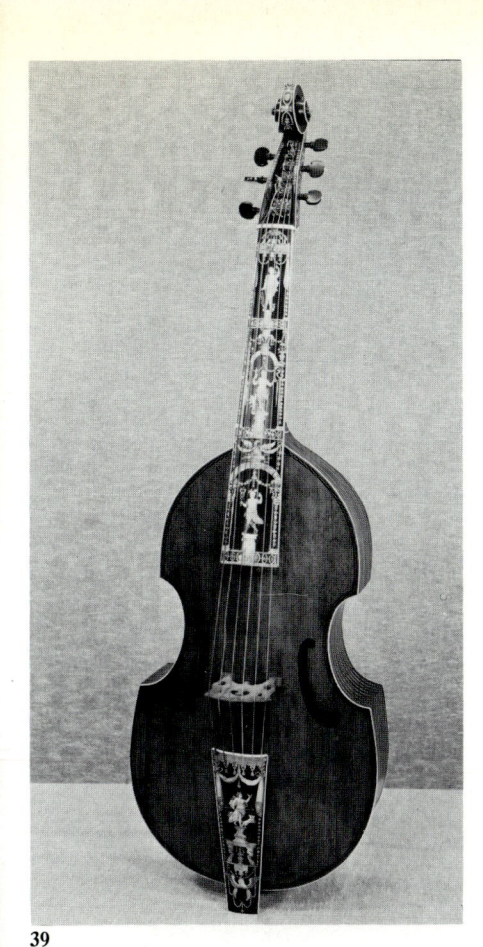

Figures 39 and 39a
A bass viol made in Hamburg in 1726, with highly refined inlaid decoration on the body and with superbly designed and executed marquetry on the finger-board and tail-piece, worked in ebony and mother-of-pearl. The marquetry designs are based on the engraved proposals for grotesques and *portière* compositions devised by Parisian artists like Jean Bérain, Claude Audran and Claude Gillot early in the eighteenth century. Copies of their engravings, or excellent imitations published in Augsburg, were available to decorators all over Europe by this time. Note the bird's-head finial of the bow which may be seen in Figure 39a.
Bass viol by Martin Voigt, Hamburg, 1726; Museum No.1298-1871.

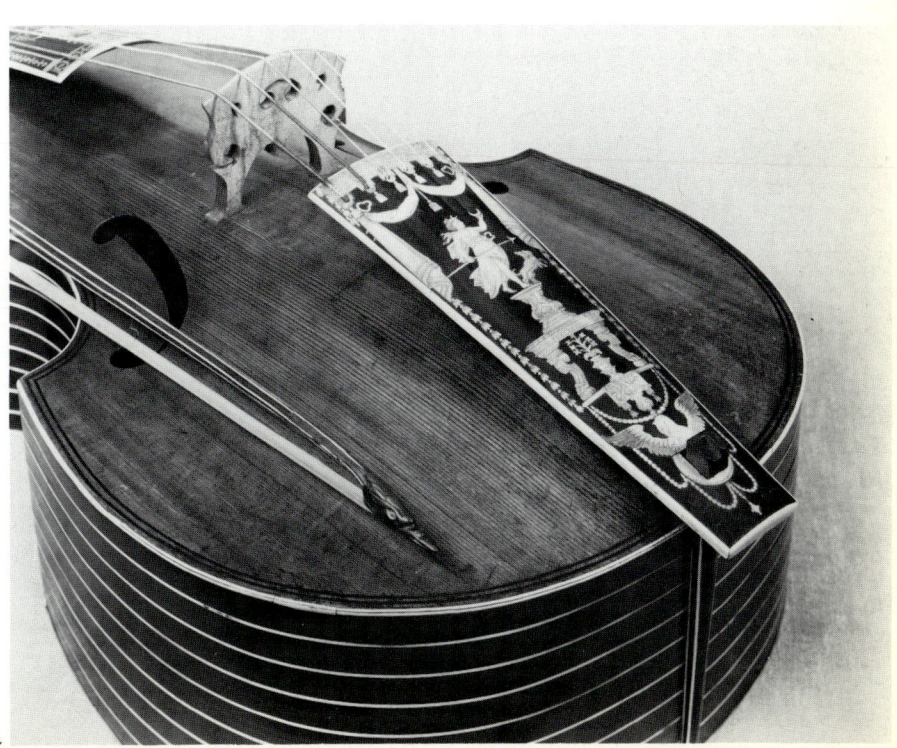

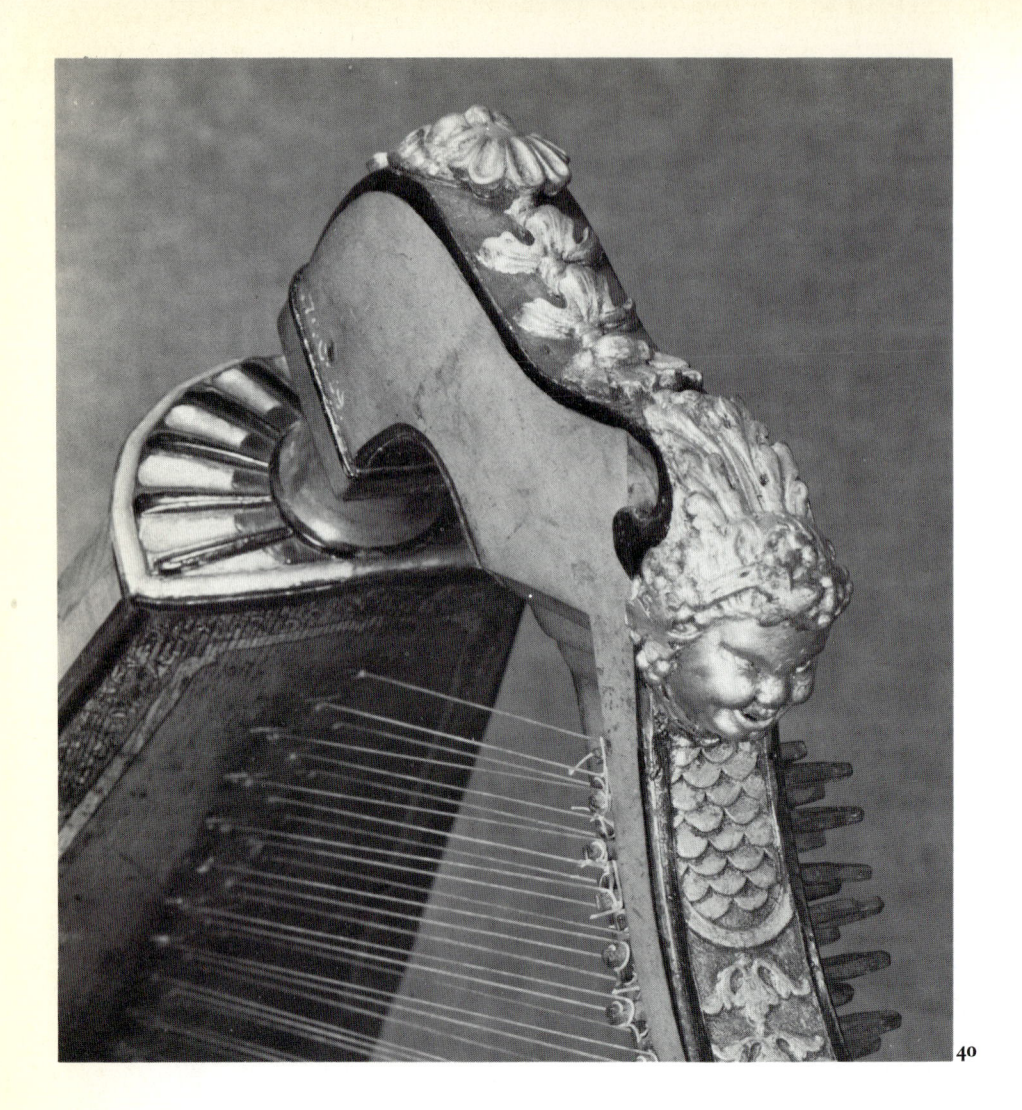

Figure 40
The neck of an elaborately decorated high-headed triple harp, made in London in 1736. The maker, David Evans, may have been identical with the harpist of that name who was in the service of George III. This harp has been associated traditionally with Charles II but the date, which was discovered in the 1960s, shows that it actually dates from the time of George II; the decoration is in fact consonant with the sort of ornament then being applied to sumptuous furniture under the influence of the architect William Kent.
Harp by David Evans, London, 1736; Museum No.1740-186a.

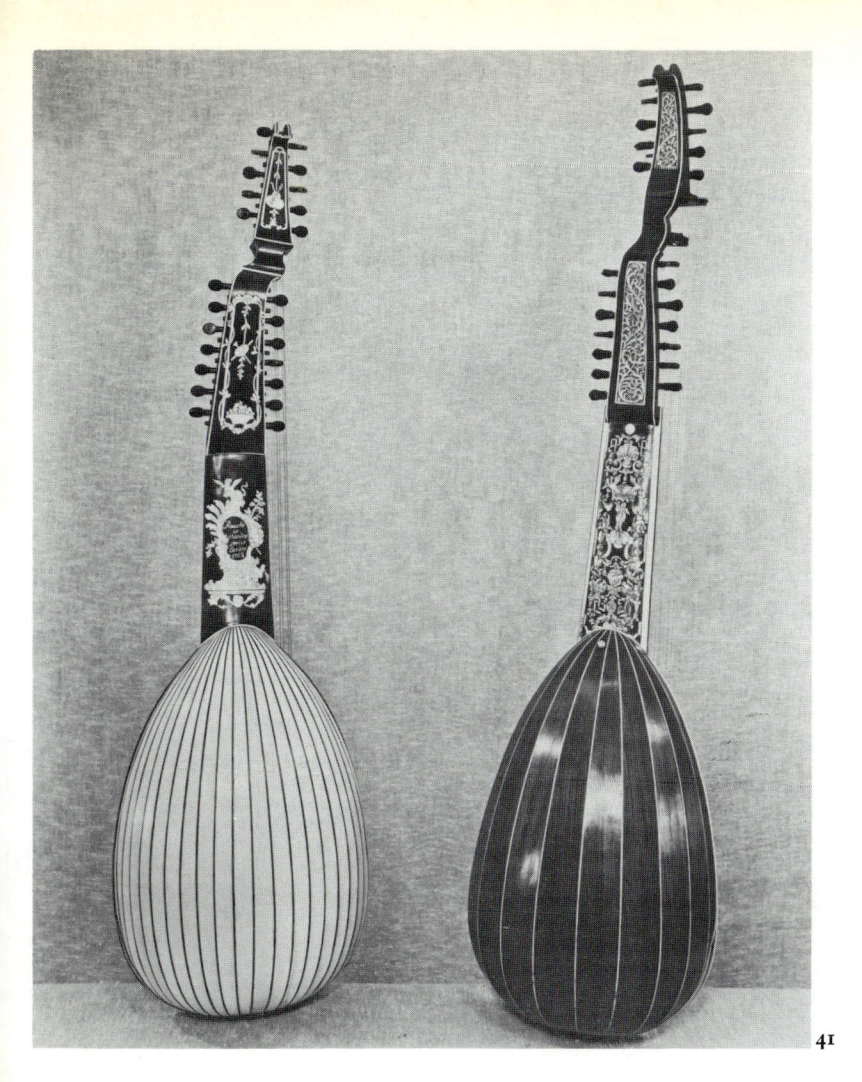

Figure 41
The theorbo enjoyed a certain amount of favour in fashionable circles in the middle decades of the eighteenth century, although other versions of the lute had by then largely fallen from favour. In order the better to suit them to their surroundings in a drawingroom, a number of these instruments were decorated in a particularly lavish manner, as these two specimens show. Both were made by Germans, one working in Hamburg and the other as an immigrant in London. That on the left bears the maker's name, (Michael) Rauche of Chandos Street, and the date 1762, all within a delightful Rococo cartouche. The whole instrument is of ivory with ebony details.
Left: Theorbo by M. Rauche, London, 1762; Museum No.9-1871.
Right: Theorbo by Heinrich Goldt, Hamburg, 1734; Museum No.4274-1856.

Figure 42
The front and back of the neck of the Goldt theorbo (see Fig.41) with *Laub und Bandelwerk* ornament executed in marquetry of ivory and tortoiseshell. As one would expect there is still no trace of Rococo ornament in this instrument which is dated 1734.

Figure 43
Two mid eighteenth century mandores, ancestors of the mandolin. Although one is Venetian and the other Parisian, both follow the traditional form established in Italy for instruments of this kind. The lower instrument has a rose that is still in the Gothic style – an astonishing example of conservatism, especially from the hands of one of the most prominent and fashionable instrument makers in Paris, at a time when novelty was of much consequence.
Above: mandore by Joseph Molinari, Venice, 1757; Museum No.19-1882.
Below: mandore by Jean-Nicholas Lambert, Paris, 1752;
Museum No.503-1865.

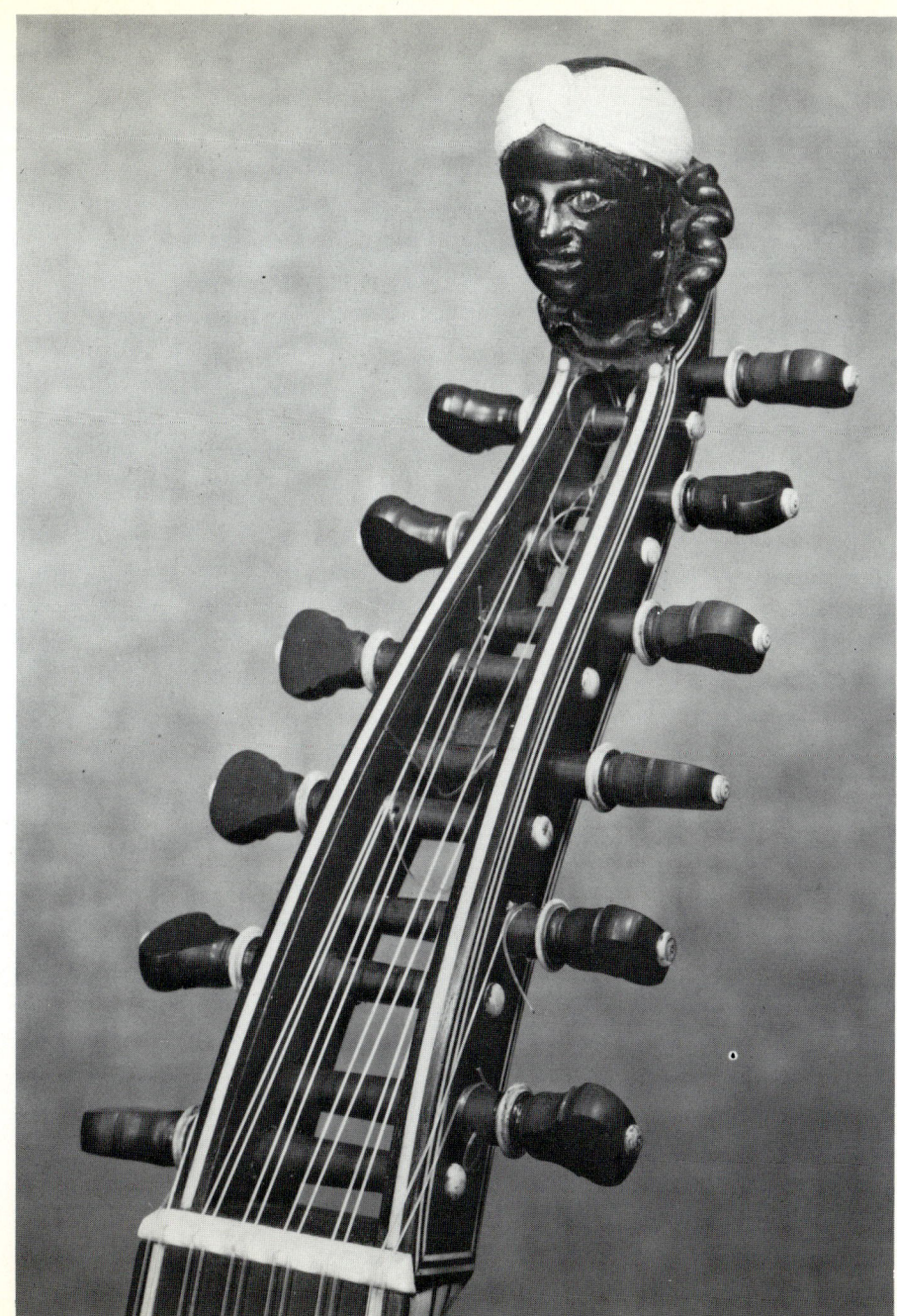

Figure 44
The peg-box and finial of the Lambert mandore (see Fig.43).

Figure 45
The inside of the lid of a large German mid eighteenth-century clavichord, painted in tones of blue with scenes of a stag hunt – perhaps rather a surprising choice of subject in the circumstances. The lids of German keyboard instruments were not normally painted with scenes at this period.
Clavichord by Barthold Fritz, Brunswick, 1751; Museum No.339-1882.

Figure 46
English keyboard instruments were commonly veneered with walnut, even when mahogany had become the fashionable wood for furniture produced in London and the chief provincial centres. The instruments were, moreover, usually left rather plain, relying on clean lines, a pleasing choice of veneers, cross-banded borders and showy brass hinges and hooks for their aesthetic appeal. Only on the nameboard would there normally be ornament, painted or executed in marquetry. The nameboard of this English spinet has exceptionally elaborate marquetry embellishment. Spinets of this characteristic wing-shaped form were extremely popular with those who could afford such things; they were roughly the equivalent of the Victorian upright piano. They were exported in considerable quantity and the reticent style of their decoration, which was shared by English harpsichords, influenced the appearance of keyboard instruments in other countries during the last decades of the century and well into the next.
Spinet by John Crang, London, 1758; Museum No.w.16-1947.

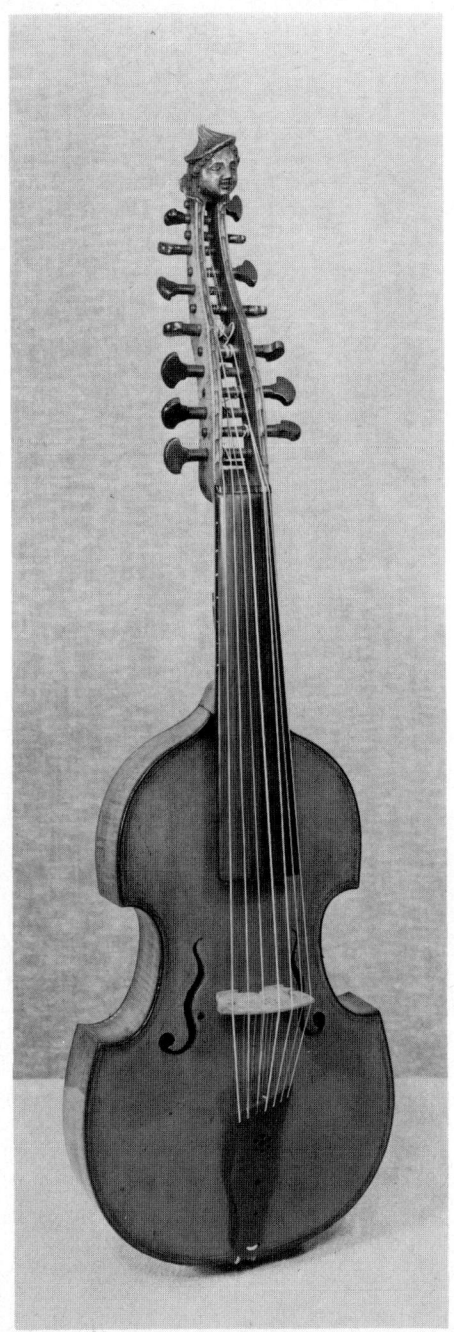

Figures 47 and 47a
A Parisian viola d'amore of unusually pleasing form. The viola d'amore, with its long peg-box (required to hold both the main and the sympathetic strings), usually had a finial in the shape of a head.
Viola d'amore from the workshops of Nicholas Lambert (when his widow was running the concern), Paris, 1772; Museum No.W.344-1921.

Figure 48
A *serinette* or bird-organ, fitted inside a casket decorated with marquetry of high quality, and embellished with ormolu mounts. It is only about 21.5 cm. high. It bears the stamp of the Parisian cabinetmaker, Leonard Boudin (master in 1761, died 1804), who produced a wide variety of furniture for a fashionable market of a somewhat conservative nature. The Neo-Classical elements in the decoration suggest that the owner was aware of the new taste that was replacing the waywardness of the Rococo or *Louis Quinze* style, and yet the Classicism is measured and unobtrusive. This is characteristic of the phase of Parisian Neo-Classicism which developed about 1770.
Bird-organ, case by Boudin, Paris, about 1770; Museum No.629-1868.

Figures 49 and 49a
This small French harpsichord is a superb piece of furniture in its own right. It is dated 1786 and, like the Vaudry harpsichord of 1681 (see colour plate section), is important as a documented specimen of Parisian japanning. It has a very narrow compass and was evidently specially commissioned, probably for the small daughter of a father who must have been wealthy, since the instrument would have been very expensive indeed. Unfortunately we know nothing of its early history. While the instrument itself was provided by the foremost Parisian harpsichord-maker, the casework must have been created by some of the best artists in the decorative field; a joiner, a carver, a gilder and a japanner will have been involved in its construction. The outside of the case is black, the inside salmon-pink.
Harpsichord by Pascal Taskin, Paris, 1786; Museum No.1121-1869.

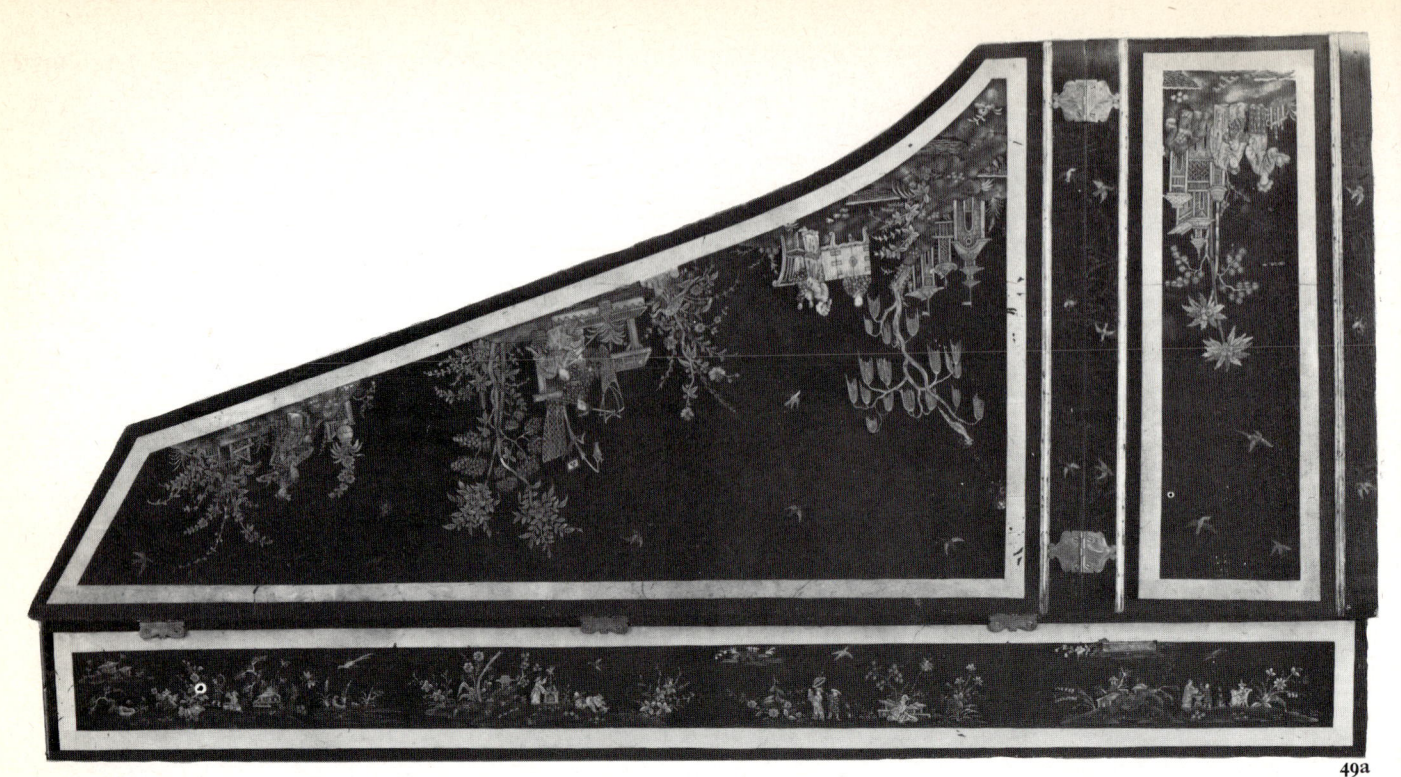

The case of the Taskin harpsichord, Figure 49.

49a

Figures 50 and 50a
Much attention was paid to the decoration of the Parisian pedal-harp which became a highly fashionable instrument during the second half of the eighteenth century. Not readily portable, such instruments stood around in grand rooms and had to blend with the prevailing *décor*. They were therefore often elegantly carved and painted. Here are two details of a particularly fine specimen made about 1785.
(Pedal-harp by H. Nadermann, Paris, about 1785; Museum No.4449-1858).

51

51a

Figures 51 and 51a
Another Parisian pedal-harp, in this case painted with musical trophies taken from J. G. Delafosse's sixth *Livre de Trophées d'Amour et Musique*. Painted decoration by the same hand is found on a number of French pedal-harps, indicating that there was a painter to whom the harp-makers could regularly turn when they wanted their harps decorated. Evidently the carved decoration on the heads of such harps was also often executed in the workshop of a craftsman who specialised in such work.

This harp is decorated with the head of a sphinx. An inscription on the harp indicates that it was made not long after 1785, and it is, therefore, a very early specimen of the use of an Egyptian motif on a piece of fashionable Parisian furniture. Egyptian motifs were, of course, used occasionally throughout the second half of the eighteenth century, but the main phase of 'the Egyptian taste' was not to arrive until the style was brought to widespread attention by the publication in 1802 of Denon's *Voyage dans la Basse et Haute Egypte pendant les Campagnes du Général Bonaparte*.
Pedal-harp by H. Nadermann, Paris, made soon after 1785; Museum No.425-1884.

Figure 52
This harp is decorated with japanned ornament on a black ground like that on the Taskin harpsichord of 1786. Chinoiserie decoration enjoyed waves of favour in fashionable circles, and a significant wave swept through Paris in the 1780s.
Pedal-harp by Wolter, Paris, about 1785; Museum No.W.46-1911.

Figure 53
A square pianoforte made in Madrid about 1815. It has a case of mahogany set with small roundels consisting of carved ivory figures on a blue ground under domed glass covers. These were presumably intended to look like Wedgwood blue and white jasperware plaques, which enjoyed widespread favour during the last decades of the eighteenth-century. A curious and sumptuously decorated Broadwood piano, with a case apparently designed for it by Thomas Sheraton (the original drawing survives), was presented to the Queen of Spain in 1796 by the Spanish prime-minister of the day. This instrument was embellished with Wedgwood plaques and it may be that its decoration to some extent inspired that of the present instrument.
Square piano by Flórez, Madrid, early nineteenth century; Museum No.48-1876.

Figure 54
A so-called 'giraffe piano', the frame of which is set upright instead of horizontally. The form was popular in Vienna and this instrument should probably be seen as a Dutch copy of a Viennese model rather than a late manifestation of the Napoleonic *Empire* style which was popular for a short while in Dutch court circles when Louis Bonaparte was on the throne (from 1808). The instrument later belonged to Sir William Orchardson (1832-1910) who depicted it in two of his paintings and later presented it to the Museum.
Giraffe piano by Van der Does, Amsterdam, about 1820; Museum No.461-1907.

Figure 55
The principal maker of harps in this country during the last century was the firm of Sebastian & Pierre Erard. Their early model was decorated in the Classical style and was called the 'Grecian Harp' but a new, 'Gothic' model was introduced in the 1830s and remained popular for a long while. The scroll beneath the angel tells us that the design was first published in December 1833. The serial number, when checked against the firm's ledgers, shows that this instrument was made in 1858.
Pedal-harp by S. & P. Erard, London, 1858; Museum No.W.48-1931.

Figures 56 and 56a
The front and back of a Spanish guitar made in the 1840s. Although the figures are shown wearing seventeenth-century costume, the hair-style of the woman betrays the true date – as is so often the case with figures in pastiches painted during the last century. Nor could any seventeenth-century artist possibly have conceived expressions of such sugary sentimentality.
Guitar from the Altimira factory, Barcelona, about 1840; Museum No.W.15-1915.

Figures 57 and 57a
The grand piano became massive and rather ungainly during the third quarter of the nineteenth-century and eventually efforts were made to disguise its shape, and to devise suitable forms of decoration. Inspiration was sought from the past, Flemish and Italian instruments of the seventeenth-century providing significant precedents. The instrument shown here has a case with a shape inspired by the harpsichord. The general concept of its decoration was sketched by Burne-Jones, and the ornament was executed in silvered and gilded gesso on a green-stained ground by Kate Faulkner of William Morris's firm in 1883.
Grand pianoforte by Broadwood in collaboration with Morris & Co., 1883;
Museum No.w.23-1927.

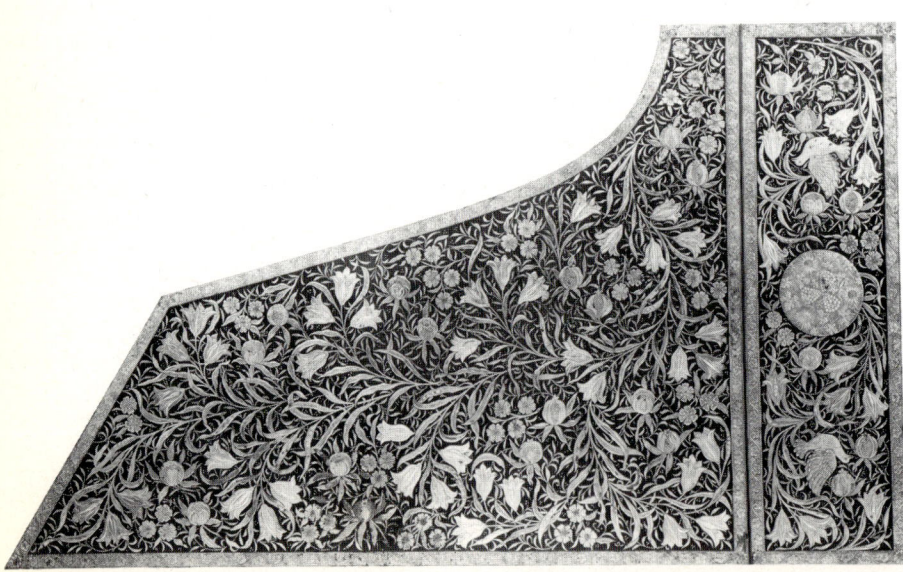

57

57a

50

Figure 58
A grand piano made in 1868-9 for the first Director of the Victoria and Albert Museum, Sir Henry Cole, who clearly enjoyed music and worked enthusiastically for the establishment of the institution which eventually became the Royal College of Music. The case is of varnished wood, stained by a process then called xylatechnigraphy. The piano was shown at the International Exhibition of 1871. The designs are by James Gamble who took actual instruments in the Museum's collection as models for those depicted on the case.
Grand pianoforte by Robert Wornum, 1868-9, Museum No.w.11-1913.

Figure 59
Rather different from the conscious attempts to evolve a form of decoration suitable for the new grand pianos as works of art in their own right, were the efforts of architects to disguise pianos in the various historical styles so greatly favoured during the nineteenth-century. The case of the piano shown here is in the 'reformed Gothic' style and was designed to blend with the décor of rooms embellished in the same taste.
Upright piano by Collard & Collard, the case probably designed by Charles Bevan, 1860s, Museum No.w.6-1968

Figure 60
An upright piano disguised as a cabinet. The form had been devised in 1896 by Hugh Baillie Scott, who called it his 'Manxman' pattern. This specimen dates from about 1903 when Broadwoods held an exhibition of architect-designed pianos including one designed by Scott for the Grand Duke of Hesse in this severe style, which was to have a profound influence in Germany and America. With its ebonised finish and striking patterns executed in marquetry with stained ivory embellishments, this piano looks forward to the sophisticated forms of the 'Art Deco' style, which did not come to hold the stage until the 1920s. In this piano we have an example of a musical instrument expressing a main line in the development of the decorative arts in Europe.
Upright piano by Broadwood; the case designed by Hugh Baillie Scott, about 1903; Museum No.W.15-1976.

Note: A useful recent essay on the embellishment of the piano is Michael Wilson's 'The Case of the Victorian Piano' *Victoria and Albert Museum Yearbook 3,* 1972. Otherwise very little fresh writing on this whole subject has been published so far.